# — LED BY —
# DIVINE
# DESIGN

## SEEKING FOR AND
## RECOGNIZING THE SPIRIT

# RONALD A. RASBAND

DESERET
BOOK

**Library of Congress Cataloging-in-Publication Data**

(CIP data on file)
ISBN 978-1-62972-548-2

Printed in the United States of America
Publishers Printing, Salt Lake City, UT

10   9   8   7   6   5   4   3   2   1

# CONTENTS

"ALWAYS HAVE
HIS SPIRIT"

# LET THE HOLY SPIRIT GUIDE

Throughout our lives we have had the opportunity to feel the Spirit of the Lord. That Spirit confirms truth to our hearts and minds.

Consider the words of this familiar hymn:

> *Let the Holy Spirit guide;*
> *Let him teach us what is true.*
> *He will testify of Christ,*
> *Light our minds with heaven's view.*
> ("Let the Holy Spirit Guide," *Hymns*, no. 143)

From latter-day revelation we know that the Godhead is comprised of three distinct and separate beings: our Father in Heaven; His Only Begotten Son, Jesus Christ; and the Holy Ghost. We know that "the Father has a body of flesh and bones as tangible as man's; the Son also; but the Holy Ghost has not a body of flesh and bones, but is a personage of Spirit. Were it not so, the Holy Ghost could not dwell in us" (D&C 130:22).

The Holy Ghost is crucially important in our lives. Our Father in Heaven knew that in mortality we would face challenges, tribulation, and turmoil; He knew we would wrestle with questions, disappointments, temptations, and weaknesses. To give us mortal strength and divine guidance, He provided the Holy Spirit, another name for the Holy Ghost.

The Holy Ghost binds us to the Lord. By divine assignment, He inspires, testifies, teaches, and prompts us to walk in the light of the Lord. We have the sacred responsibility to learn to recognize His influence in our lives and respond.

REMEMBER THE LORD'S PROMISE:
"I will impart unto you of my Spirit, which shall enlighten your mind, which shall fill your soul with joy" (D&C 11:13). I love that assurance. Joy that fills our souls brings with it an eternal perspective in contrast to day-to-day living. That joy comes as peace amidst hardship or heartache. It provides comfort and courage, unfolds the truths of the gospel, and expands our love for the Lord and all God's children. Although the need for such blessings is so great, in many ways the world has forgotten and forsaken them.

# HOW DO WE "ALWAYS REMEMBER HIM"?

Each week as we partake of the holy sacrament, we make a covenant to "always remember him," the Lord Jesus Christ, and His atoning sacrifice. When we keep this sacred covenant, the promise is given that we "may always have his Spirit to be with [us]" (D&C 20:77).

How do we do that?

First, we strive to live worthy of the Spirit.

The Holy Ghost accompanies those who are "strict to remember the Lord their God from day to day" (Alma 58:40). As the Lord counseled, we must "lay aside the things of this world, and seek for the things of a better" (D&C 25:10), for "the Spirit of the Lord doth not dwell in unholy temples" (Helaman 4:24). We must always try to obey God's laws, study the scriptures, pray, attend the temple, and live true to the thirteenth article of faith, "being honest, true, chaste, benevolent, virtuous, and . . . doing good to all men."

*Elder Rasband and Elder Weidner with Marti and Sister Schaffer.*

Second, we must be willing to receive the Spirit.

The Lord has promised, "I will tell you in your mind and in your heart, by the Holy Ghost, which shall come upon you and which shall dwell in your heart" (D&C 8:2). I began to understand this as a young missionary in Scotch Plains, New Jersey. One hot July morning my companion and I felt prompted to look up a Temple Square referral. We knocked on the door of the Elwood Schaffer home. Mrs. Schaffer politely turned us away.

As she began to shut the door, I felt to do something I had never done before and have never done since! I stuck my foot in the door, and I asked, "Is there anyone else who might be interested in our message?" Her sixteen-year-old daughter, Marti, did have an interest and had fervently prayed for guidance just the day before. Marti met with us, and in time her mother participated in the discussions. Both of them joined the Church.

Resulting from Marti's baptism, 136 people, including many of her own family members, have been baptized and made gospel covenants. How grateful I am that I listened to the Spirit and stuck my foot in the door on that hot July day.

Third, we must recognize the Spirit when it comes.

My experience has been that the Spirit most often communicates as a feeling. You feel it in words that are familiar to you, that make sense to you, that prompt you. Consider the response of the Nephites as they listened to the Lord pray for them: "And the multitude did hear and do bear record; and their hearts were open and they did understand in their hearts the words which he prayed" (3 Nephi 19:33). They felt in their

*Elder and Sister Rasband with Brother Weidner and Marti's family.*

hearts the words of His prayer. The voice of the Holy Spirit is still and small.

President Thomas S. Monson taught, "As we pursue the journey of life, let us learn the language of the Spirit" ("The Spirit Giveth Life," *Ensign,* May 1985). The Spirit speaks words that we feel. These feelings are gentle: a nudge to act, to do something, to say something, to respond in a certain way. If we are casual or complacent in our worship, drawn off and desensitized by worldly pursuits, we find ourselves diminished in our ability to feel. Nephi said to Laman and Lemuel, "Ye have heard his voice from time to time; and he hath spoken unto you in a still small voice, but ye were past feeling, that ye could not feel [the] words" (1 Nephi 17:45).

# ON OUR FATHER'S BUSINESS

Once, on an assignment to South America, we were on a tight ten-day schedule visiting Colombia, Peru, and Ecuador. An enormous earthquake had killed hundreds, injured tens of thousands, and damaged and destroyed homes and communities in the Ecuadorian cities of Portoviejo and Manta. We felt prompted to add to our schedule a visit to members living in those cities. With damage to the roads, we weren't sure we could get there. In fact, we had been told we could not get there, but the prompting would not go away. Consequently, we were blessed and were able to visit both cities.

With such short notice, we expected that only a few local priesthood leaders would attend the hastily organized gatherings. However, we arrived at each stake center to find the chapels filled all the way back to the stage. Some who attended were the stalwarts of the region, the pioneers who had held fast to the Church, encouraging others to join them in worship and to feel the Spirit in their lives. Sitting on the front rows were the members who had lost loved ones and neighbors in the earthquake. I was privileged to bestow an apostolic blessing upon all who were in attendance, one of my very first given. Though I was standing at the front of that room, it was as if my hands were on each of their heads, and I felt the words of the Lord pouring forth.

If we pay attention to the promptings that come to us, we will grow in the spirit of revelation and receive more and more Spirit-driven insight and direction. The Lord has said, "Put your trust in that Spirit which leadeth to do good" (D&C 11:12).

# FIRST RESPONDERS

Remember the words of Nephi: "I was led by the Spirit, not knowing beforehand the things which I should do. Nevertheless," he said, "I went forth" (1 Nephi 4:6–7).

And so must we. We must be confident in our first promptings. Sometimes we rationalize; we wonder if we are feeling a spiritual impression or if it is just our own thoughts. When we begin to second-guess, even third-guess, our feelings—and we all have—we are dismissing the Spirit; we are questioning divine counsel. The Prophet Joseph Smith taught that if you will listen to the first promptings, you will get it right nine times out of ten (see Truman G. Madsen, *Joseph Smith the Prophet* [1989], 103).

Now a caution: don't expect fireworks because you responded to the Holy Ghost. Remember, you are about the work of the still, small voice.

*Mission President Rasband with missionaries in Columbus Day parade, New York City.*

While serving as a mission president in New York City, I was with some of our missionaries in a restaurant in the Bronx. A young family came in and sat near us. They appeared golden for the gospel. I watched our missionaries as they continued to visit with me, then noticed as the family concluded their meal and slipped out the door. Then I said, "Elders, there's a lesson here today. You saw a lovely family come into this restaurant. What should we have done?"

One of the elders spoke up quickly: "I thought about getting up and going over to talk to them. I felt the nudge, but I didn't respond."

"Elders," I said, "we must always act on our first prompting. That nudge you felt was the Holy Ghost!"

First promptings are pure inspiration from heaven. When

they confirm or testify to us, we need to recognize them for what they are and never let them slip past. So often, it is the Spirit inspiring us to reach out to someone in need, family and friends in particular. "Thus . . . the still small voice, which whispereth through and pierceth all things" (D&C 85:6) points us to opportunities to teach the gospel, to bear testimony of Jesus Christ and the Restoration, to offer support and concern, and to rescue one of God's precious children.

Think of it as being what is called a first responder. In most communities the first responders to a tragedy, disaster, or calamity are firefighters, police officers, or paramedics. They arrive with lights flashing, and, may I add, we are so incredibly grateful for them. The Lord's way is less obvious but requires just as immediate a response. The Lord knows the needs of all His children—and He knows who is prepared to help. If we let the Lord know in our morning prayers that we are ready, He will call on us to respond. If we respond, He will call on us time and time again and we will find ourselves on what President Monson called "the Lord's errand" ("To Learn, to Do, to Be," *Ensign,* November 2008). We will become spiritual first responders bringing help from on high.

May we take seriously the Lord's call to "be of good cheer, for I will lead you along" (D&C 78:18). He leads us by the Holy Ghost. May we live close to the Spirit, acting quickly upon our first promptings, knowing they come from God.

SEEKING
THE SPIRIT

# A STILL SMALL VOICE

Sister Afton Pettigrew was one of the best Primary teachers I ever had! In many ways, she changed my life. Even today I still remember one special lesson she taught about the Holy Ghost when I was about eight.

I was a pretty lively child. I didn't like having to sit reverently through a whole Primary lesson. On this day, she couldn't get me to understand what or who the Holy Ghost was. To me, a ghost was a scary thing, and I thought the Holy Ghost was something to be afraid of.

Then Sister Pettigrew said, "Ronnie, I'd like to have you stand in front of the class and read a scripture for us. It's 1 Kings 19:11–12."

I didn't want to stand in front of all those Primary kids and read a scripture. But I took the Old Testament she handed to me and began to read what the Lord said to the prophet Elijah:

"Go forth, and stand upon the mount before the Lord. And, behold, the Lord passed by, and a great and strong wind rent the mountains, and brake in pieces the rocks before the Lord; but the Lord was not in the wind: and after the wind an earthquake; but the Lord was not in the earthquake:

"And after the earthquake a fire; but the Lord was not in the fire: and after the fire a still small voice."

I finished reading and looked up. Sister Pettigrew could tell I was a little confused about what I'd read, so she explained. "That means that when the Lord speaks to you, He won't speak in big, loud ways, like wind storms or earthquakes or fires. You'll hear Him speak very quietly, like a still, small voice in your heart."

Then she said, "By the way, Ronnie, you have a very pleasant voice. You read and speak very well."

I couldn't believe it! Not only did Sister Pettigrew teach me about the Holy Ghost, but she also helped me see one of my talents!

I was a changed boy after that. I learned that the Holy Ghost speaks to us through thoughts in our mind and peaceful feelings in our heart. I tried to remember to listen inside me for those thoughts and feelings. If I was doing something wrong, like not being reverent in Primary, I listened. Or if I had to make a decision about something, I listened. Sometimes the voice was very soft. I had to be quiet on the inside and on the outside to recognize it. And if I didn't listen the first time or the second time, it became softer and softer until I couldn't feel it anymore.

Listening to that still, small voice also helped me find and improve the talents Heavenly Father blessed me with.

Today as a grownup, I still think of Sister Pettigrew and how she helped me. How grateful I am for her and for all our Primary teachers all over the world who teach children how to bring Heavenly Father into their lives and how to grow their talents.

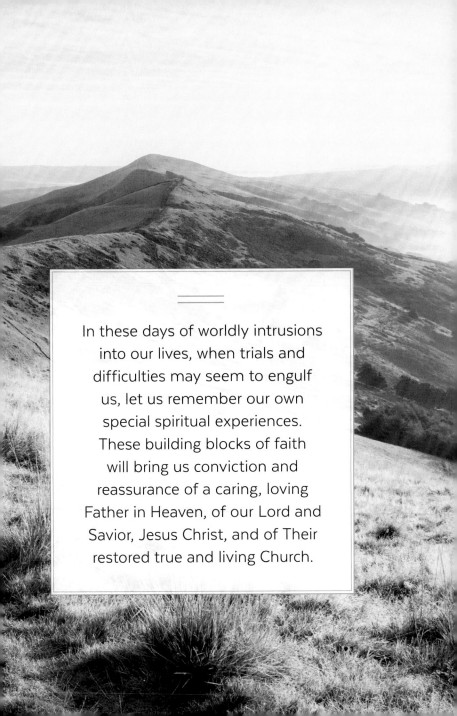

In these days of worldly intrusions into our lives, when trials and difficulties may seem to engulf us, let us remember our own special spiritual experiences. These building blocks of faith will bring us conviction and reassurance of a caring, loving Father in Heaven, of our Lord and Savior, Jesus Christ, and of Their restored true and living Church.

# CONSTANT COMPANIONSHIP OF THE HOLY GHOST

Through confirmation and by the laying on of hands, you have already been given the gift of the Holy Ghost. As it states in Doctrine and Covenants 39:23, "And again, it shall come to pass that on as many as ye shall baptize with water, ye shall lay your hands, and they shall receive the gift of the Holy Ghost." This will be a great privilege for you throughout your life to have this special gift from the Lord.

Enjoying the constant companionship of the Holy Ghost is quite a different matter—and a goal for all of us to try and achieve.

Anger, disunity, contention, lying, and impurity of thoughts and deeds, to name a few vices, chase away the holy presence of this third member of the Godhead. Such unaltered and unrepentant behavior causes Latter-day Saints to lose the Spirit and lose confidence.

Let us take improper thoughts, even immoral thoughts, as an example. From the Doctrine and Covenants we read, "And verily I say unto you, as I have said before, he that looketh on a woman to lust after her, or if any shall commit adultery in their hearts, they shall not have the Spirit" (D&C 63:16).

I would offer you a little formula that you can remember easily, that almost certainly will enable you to have the Spirit as your constant companion.

First, bridle your passions. Let us look at Alma's teachings to his son Shiblon, who was beginning his mission:

"And now, as ye have begun to teach the word even so I would that ye should continue to teach; and I would that ye would be diligent and temperate in all things.

"See that ye are not lifted up unto pride; yea, see that ye do not boast in your own wisdom, nor of your much strength.

"Use boldness, but not overbearance; and also see that ye bridle all your passions, that ye may be filled with love; see that ye refrain from idleness" (Alma 38:10–12).

I would like to focus on the word *bridle.* To bridle our passions is a remarkable caution the Lord gave the prophet Alma in the Book of Mormon. A wild horse needs to be "broken" or trained to succumb to the will of its master. A bridle or harness is used for this purpose. It is also used thereafter to guide and restrain the animal. Similarly, our natural passions need to be broken so that we can likewise follow the will of our Master, even the Lord Jesus Christ. Passions, like wild horses, need to be bridled and restrained as we strive to be obedient and follow the Lord's teachings.

In a worldly environment such as the one in which we live, which could suggest one can have everything now, bridling our passions in terms of our physical yearnings is mandatory. We just must do it.

*Horse with bridle.*

Some examples that people might be facing could be:

- Staying out too late.
- Watching inappropriate movies, DVDs, or television shows.
- Being obsessed with video or internet games.
- Playing popular games of chance, like poker.
- Indulging to any degree in pornography.

All of these are examples of natural man or woman passions and the adversary's temptations that need to be bridled.

From the Doctrine and Covenants we find and read the second part of the formula: "garnish your thoughts":

"Let thy bowels also be full of charity towards all men, and to the household of faith, and let virtue garnish thy thoughts unceasingly; then shall thy confidence wax strong in the presence of God. . . .

"The Holy Ghost shall be thy constant companion" (D&C 121:45–46).

The Lord uses another fascinating phrase here: to let virtue garnish our thoughts unceasingly. In other words, to enhance or embellish our thoughts with virtue. I think of a common garnishment as an addition to a nice plate of food. The garnish adds beauty and delight to the meal, just as virtue does to our thoughts.

So what does it mean for us to garnish our thoughts with virtue? There are several helpful references in the scriptures, including the thirteenth article of faith: "We believe in being honest, true, chaste, benevolent, virtuous, and in doing good to all men; indeed, we may say that we follow the admonition of Paul—We believe all things, we hope all things, we have endured many things and hope to be able to endure all things. If there is anything virtuous, lovely or of good report or praiseworthy, we seek after these things."

Alma taught that in resisting temptation we can draw upon the scriptures to increase our personal virtue and strength: "And now, as the preaching of the word had a great tendency to lead the people to do that which was just—yea, it had had more powerful effect upon the minds of the people than the sword, or anything else, which had happened unto them—therefore

Alma thought it was expedient that they should try the virtue of the word of God" (Alma 31:5).

Paul, in writing to the Philippians, also advised: "Finally, brethren, whatsoever things are true, whatsoever things are honest, whatsoever things are just, whatsoever things are pure, whatsoever things are lovely, whatsoever things are of good report; if there be any virtue, and if there be any praise, think on these things" (Philippians 4:8).

It has been my experience that very little occurs in the way of transgression that is not first rehearsed and debated in one's own mind and soul. A huge key in avoiding these pitfalls is to let virtue be in our thoughts and deeds always, not allowing our minds to wander. I can recommend it without reservation as a way to flee from temptation and transgression.

The third part of this formula is that we must ask for the Spirit—pray for it.

From Doctrine and Covenants 63:64, "Remember that that which cometh from above is sacred, and must be spoken with care, and by constraint of the Spirit; and in this there is no condemnation, and ye receive the Spirit through prayer."

"Ye receive the Spirit through prayer." I have seen so many missionaries humbly kneeling, sweet appealing for the power of the Spirit. Our Father has provided, in His plan of happiness, a Savior for us, even Christ the Lord. Through self-control and repentance, we can each tame the natural men and women that we are.

I invite you to consider your passions and, where necessary, bridle them in your life.

I invite you to bridle your thoughts and garnish them with virtue, such as that found in the beloved word of God.

I invite you to humbly and prayerfully plead with the Lord to bless you with the Holy Ghost.

I invite you to go before the Lord and ask Him to bless you with strength. I promise you, as a servant of the Lord, that He will bless you with the presence and companionship of the Holy Ghost. Bridle your passions and garnish your thoughts, and by the prayer of faith you will be led by the Spirit and join in this magnificent miracle.

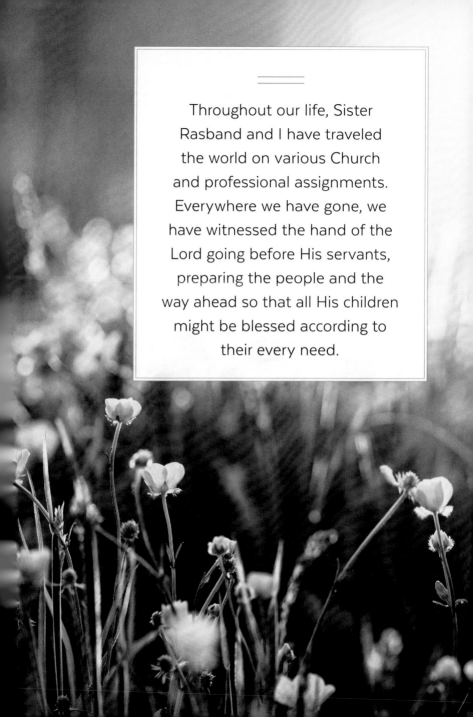

Throughout our life, Sister Rasband and I have traveled the world on various Church and professional assignments. Everywhere we have gone, we have witnessed the hand of the Lord going before His servants, preparing the people and the way ahead so that all His children might be blessed according to their every need.

# STRENGTH TO REMAIN TRUE

A key element in having the Spirit with us in our lives is remaining true to the light we have received. This is becoming increasingly difficult in a world of differing values.

Protecting conscience is about safeguarding the way someone thinks and feels and their right to act on those beliefs. I am talking about someone telling you that the thoughts, feelings, and beliefs you have are not allowed, valued, or acceptable because your views are not popular. A war in heaven was fought for agency, and it is a gross violation of that agency to force someone to betray their conscience because their views do not align with the crowd.

The Lord does not give us a free pass to live any way we choose without consequences. We are still accountable to Him for our choices. He has said, "Be ye therefore perfect, even as your Father which is in heaven is perfect" (Matthew 5:48). The commandment to seek after perfection implies that we start where we are and seek the Lord's help to lift us to where He wants us to go. Being true to our authentic self requires continual effort to increase our light, knowledge, and understanding.

The Savior demonstrated perfectly how to reach out in love and encouragement while also holding firm to what we know to be true. Remember that when the woman was caught in adultery, the Lord asked for anyone without sin to step forward and be the first to condemn her. When no one approached, our Savior, who was without sin, commented, "Neither do I condemn thee: go, and sin no more" (John 8:11). The forgiveness and kindness He showed her did not contradict His teachings that sexual intimacy is meant for a husband and a wife who are legally and lawfully married. You too can be unyielding in right and truth yet still reach out in kindness.

When you feel completely and perfectly loved, it is much easier to love others and to see them the way the Savior does. Please turn to our Savior in prayer and ask to receive His pure love both for yourself and for others. He has promised that you will feel His love if you ask in faith.

IN FAMILIES

# TRUST THE LORD
# IN MARRIAGE

In 1976, I was the elders quorum president in my campus ward, and Brother Jon Huntsman was the high council adviser. He was already successful in his plastics business. I even remember him slipping me a personal check for $1,000 with these simple instructions: "Use this to help those who are in need in your quorum." They were never to know where the money came from.

After a year of working with him in that ecclesiastical setting, I was surprised one day when he asked me to come to his office. There I was in plush, professional business surroundings—me, the son of a truck driver—when Jon invited me to join his company working in marketing and sales. I was honored. Sister Rasband and I had been praying for meaningful employment after graduation. We had a young family, and we were living on meager funds.

Jon explained that he was not interested in my academic credentials—which were not stellar—but that he had seen my strengths of leadership and character that were a good fit for his business. Those traits he observed were a strong work ethic and an ability to juggle the pressures of family, education, work, and Church service. I learned that they were his best traits.

I immediately responded that his offer was an answer to prayer and that I would love to join his company after graduation in the spring. My college degree was so important to me, my wife, and my parents.

He smiled and then said, "I need you now." Next week, he explained, he would be in Troy, Ohio, at one of his packaging plants to negotiate with a major customer. If I wanted the job, I needed to be with him as the new account manager. That was it. The job was next week or no job at all.

That night, after seeking counsel from loved ones and friends, Sister Rasband and I prayed earnestly for direction. My dear wife, Melanie, was inspired with our answer. "Isn't this what people go to college for, to find an opportunity like this one?" she asked.

We agreed that it was. The Spirit confirmed our decision, and we took the job in Ohio.

I left the campus of the University of Utah just two semesters short of receiving my degree. Eleven years later I was

*Ron and Melanie Rasband in 1973, when they were married.*

surprised and humbled again when Jon Huntsman appointed me president of his global corporation, with thousands of employees and billions in revenues—and still without that college degree! I am not recommending that anyone skip that last, important step in his or her education. But this should suggest that there is a masterpiece within each one of us, and when spiritually nurtured, carefully mentored, and loyally engaged in building up our families and the Lord's kingdom, all things are possible.

What did I learn from that beginning? I learned that marriage is a partnership and that you and your wife or husband are facing life together. For each of you, your spouse will sometimes get the inspiration for both of you. That is what happened in this launch of my business career. Sister Rasband and I learned early to counsel together. That spiritual aspect of our relationship, and our trust in the Lord, has been our foundation for many years.

"Keep thy soul diligently, lest thou forget the things which thine eyes have seen, and lest they depart from thy heart all the days of thy life: but teach them thy sons, and thy sons' sons" (Deuteronomy 4:9).

Generations are affected by the choices we make. Share your testimony with your family; encourage them to remember how they felt when they recognized the Spirit in their lives and to record those feelings in journals and personal histories so that their own words may, when needed, bring to their remembrance how good the Lord has been to them.

# THE SPIRIT OF THE TEMPLE

Those who are seeking the Spirit will often be led to the temple. What temples bring to families and individuals seeking to draw closer to the Lord Jesus Christ and our Father in Heaven, seeking peace in a fractured world, seeking comfort in times of trouble, cannot be calculated. Let me give you a personal example.

When I was called to serve in the Area Presidency in England, my wife, Melanie, and I quickly realized what a sacrifice it would be for our five children, especially the two youngest, who would move with us. Being uprooted is not easy. Our son in particular was looking forward to his last year of high school and all the athletic competitions that he would now miss.

Once we arrived in England, we tried to help them feel at home and at peace in a foreign land. One day, when we were assigned to speak at the Missionary Training Center in

*Elder and Sister Rasband with daughter Shannon and son Christian
at the Missionary Training Center in Preston, England, 2000.*

Preston, England, the temple president invited us to come over to the temple nearby. We accepted his invitation and soon determined that we wanted to bring our children with us to do baptisms for the dead. That was not something we had done in our busy life back home. Off we went to the north, spending the day at a temple that was, in some ways, foreign to us as well. The minute we walked into the temple baptistry, everything changed. We knew the Spirit. We knew we were home.

And then the miracle. Our children looked at us as we left that sacred place and commented how cool it had been. Then they said with sincerity, "Dad, why haven't we done this as a family before?"

I learned a lesson that day. The power of the temple had changed our perspectives. As a family, we had been sanctified by the spirit of the temple. We had felt peace and joy that no football tournament or basketball game could bring. We had stepped away from the world and been spiritually lifted.

# BOUND IN LOVE THROUGH FAMILY HISTORY

The blessings of temple service are generational. We know as Latter-day Saints that temple and family history work is pertinent to our salvation. This work is also instrumental in connecting us and our families with the Spirit of the Lord. We refer to the feelings that we can have in seeking out our departed ancestors as having the spirit of Elijah.

President James E. Faust said about this work: "Searching for our kindred dead isn't just a hobby. It is a fundamental responsibility for all members of the Church. We believe that life continues after death and that all will be resurrected. We believe that families may continue in the next life if they have kept the special covenants made in one of the sacred temples under the authority of God. We believe that our deceased ancestors can also be eternally united with their families when we make covenants in their behalf in the temples. Our deceased forebears may accept these covenants, if they choose to do so, in the spirit world" ("The Phenomenon That Is You," *Ensign,* November 2003).

I encourage you to spend time together searching for information about your ancestors on the internet; you can do that at home with little children running about; then you can take those family members to the temple and do their temple work. They may not be able to speak to you directly, but you may feel them with you, and their gratitude will be without words. The Spirit attends this work and will fill the lives of those who engage in it.

WITH FRIENDS
AND COLLEAGUES

# INSPIRED FRIENDS
# AND MENTORS

Often the Spirit works in our lives through the instrumentality of other people. Some friends are wise and trusted mentors. They are a special kind of friend; they have gone before us, and they know the way. The Spirit can direct them to offer their help in our journey. A more experienced, trusted individual can serve as an effective guide and adviser to a less experienced person, helping to shape that person's understanding and teaching principles that will make him or her more effective, stronger, wiser, and more valuable as a servant of God.

Pause for a minute and think: Who has mentored you? What have you learned from them that is life changing? How have they watched over you? How will you take their example and be a mentor yourself to family members, friends, and colleagues—those who may need and desire such a relationship?

When Sister Rasband and I were called to preside over the New York New York North Mission, we enjoyed the privilege of working with many faithful missionaries. Not only were we able to help them be more effective in their current callings as servants of the Lord Jesus Christ, but our connection has continued to this day as we assist them with letters of recommendation, counsel, encouragement, and all of our love. The Spirit has guided us to be a blessing to them as others have been for us.

There are many potential friends and mentors available to you. Let me suggest a few: bishops, stake presidents, mission presidents, quorum leaders, professors, seminary and institute teachers, youth leaders, trusted friends and colleagues, Relief Society sisters, and so many others. I have benefited from so many of their examples and teachings, and so have you! Take full advantage of their ideas, and let their influence inspire and bless your life too.

Ralph Waldo Emerson gave great counsel when he observed, "The only way to have a friend is to be one" (Ralph Waldo Emerson, "Friendship," *Essays: First Series* [1841]). And the old cliché "Birds of a feather flock together" is still true. To have friends who live high standards, who stand for virtue and goodness, who are faithful and true to their covenants, you must be such a person to them.

# INTEGRITY OPENS HEARTS TO THE SPIRIT

Regardless of your age, you are learning skills that will help you establish traditions in your homes and families, methods in your work, and contributions to society in general. Skill is important, but hearts guide hands. Jesus counseled His disciples, "Wherefore, settle this in your hearts, that ye will do the things which I shall teach, and command you" (Joseph Smith Translation, Luke 14:28 [Luke 14:27, footnote b]).

Acting with integrity invites the Spirit into our lives. I saw that in my employer and mentor, Jon Huntsman. His heart was not hardened by hardship or sin, wounds of the past, or imperfect people. Most important, his word was his bond.

Let me give you an example. Back in the 1980s, our young business was struggling. Earnings had plummeted in the recession. Jon decided to sell 40 percent of the company. He found a buyer, and, after tough negotiations, the two fixed a price and shook hands on the deal. Six months went by while the

*Ron Rasband and Jon Huntsman in Ribécourt, France.*

necessary papers, contracts, and terms were completed to provide a legally binding arrangement.

During that period the market turned. Our company's earnings climbed; sales exceeded all previous levels. Wall Street analysts advised that the 40 percent agreed to earlier was now worth five times the original amount, and the lawyers took the position that the oral agreement was not binding, since no papers had been signed.

The buyers, realizing the dramatic growth of the company, expected to pay a much higher price. There was no question that we needed that extra capital as the company expanded.

But Jon was a man of his word, and his handshake was no casual commitment. He informed the buyers of his decision to honor the original agreement and shocked the chemical industry. He would lose millions in the deal, but to him, a deal was a deal. His handshake was his bond.

Integrity in business and in spiritual and family matters all draw from the same well of strength—our love for the Lord Jesus Christ.

# JESUS CHRIST, OUR TRUEST FRIEND

In my youth, an inspired patriarch laid his hands on my head and by revelation opened to me an understanding of my potential—for who I really am—and gave a direction for my life, just like a patriarch has done for most of you. I was told that I would not lack for friends and associates, that their friendship would be a special blessing to me both temporally as well as spiritually. I was counseled to select for my closest friends those who were righteous and had a desire to keep the commandments of God. Then, as now, I realized the importance of good friends in helping me stay close to the Spirit.

As we think of friendship, think of what the Prophet Joseph Smith saw in a vision and recorded of the Apostles preaching in England: "I saw the Twelve Apostles of the Lamb, who are now upon the earth, who hold the keys of this last ministry, in foreign lands, standing together in a circle, much fatigued, with their clothes tattered and feet swollen, with their eyes cast downward, and Jesus standing in their midst, and they did not behold Him. The Savior looked upon them and wept" ("History, 1838–1856, volume B-1 [1 September 1834–2 November 1838]," 696, *The Joseph Smith Papers,* http://www .josephsmithpapers.org/paper-summary/history-1838-1856 -volume-b-1-1-september-1834-2-november-1838/150).

Though they did not see Him, Jesus stood by them. Aware of their plight and sympathetic to their hardship, it was His loving support that sustained them in their mission and brought hundreds and thousands of new converts into the Church. It was the Savior who said to His disciples, "Ye are my friends" (D&C 84:63). It was the Savior who taught, "Greater love hath no man than this, that a man lay down his life for his friends" (John 15:13). It was the Savior who beckoned, "Come unto me" (Matthew 11:28). In friendship, as in every other principle of the gospel, Jesus Christ is our Exemplar.

IN CHURCH
SERVICE

From my earliest days in Primary, I have always loved the stories of the Old Testament. Though these stories at times seemed supernatural to me with their portrayals of divine intervention in the affairs of God's children, they are, first of all, accounts of the lives of otherwise ordinary men and women. Noah, Ruth, Jeremiah, Esther, and many others dealt with challenges that are the common lot of mankind: they married, had children, worked to survive, confronted enemies, battled discouragement, and in the process had their lives touched by God in often spectacular ways.

In reading about these Old Testament individuals, we discover that they were not so different from us. The fact that God was mindful of them and that they were of service to Him gives hope that the same is possible for us.

# DIVINE GUIDANCE IN USING OUR TALENTS FOR THE LORD'S WORK

As you learn to be led by the Spirit, may I suggest that you first *seek earnestly to discover the talents the Lord has given you.* The Spirit will help you know how you can use those gifts in the Lord's service.

The talents God has given us first become apparent in the interests we pursue. If you are wondering about your talents, make a list of the things you like to do. Include all the activities you enjoy from different dimensions of your life—spiritual, musical, dramatic, academic, athletic, and so on. Study and ponder your patriarchal blessing for insights and inspiration. Consult family members, trusted friends, teachers, and leaders; others often can see in us what we find difficult to see in ourselves.

Eldred G. Smith, former Patriarch to the Church, gave this wonderful counsel: "Everyone has inherent talents. From a study of your [Family History] genealogy, find the talents you have inherited by the things you like to do, and do easily, that some of your ancestors have done. Then become an expert or a specialist in some phase of that field. The Lord will bless your efforts in your studies and in your daily work" ("Decision," *Ensign,* May 1978).

In this day and time, when family history work has become so accessible to everyone, it would be well to look into the lives of your ancestors. Perhaps you will find a vast amount of information that will help you in recognizing the gifts and talents you have been blessed with. In many cases, you will find that you have many of the same talents as those who have gone on before.

President Spencer W. Kimball said: "God has endowed us with talents and time, with latent abilities and with opportunities to use and develop them in His service. He therefore expects much of us, his privileged children" (*The Miracle of Forgiveness* [1969], 100).

Let me reassure you, each one of you has been blessed with special talents. Each of you has been blessed with divine talents by our Father in Heaven. He is waiting for you to identify, develop, and magnify those talents He has blessed you with.

As a nineteen-year-old missionary, I yearned to know if I had been blessed with any helpful missionary-related talents. I felt a great desire to know how I could magnify whatever gifts I had so that I could be a more effective servant of the

*Elder Rasband as a nineteen-year-old missionary.*

Lord. As I studied the scriptures and my patriarchal blessing, prayed fervently, and had various missionary experiences, several of my talents were made known to me. These talents, identified and strengthened as a missionary, bless me in my ministry to this very day.

Next, *use your talents to build up the kingdom of God,* and I don't just mean the Church. Our first priority in building the kingdom is helping others in our own family. Parents are in a unique and powerful position to encourage and support their children in developing their talents. Siblings, aunts, uncles, cousins, extended family members; we all have many opportunities to help others identify their talents. I am grateful for the many people who have helped me add to my talents. The successes in life of those we assist, sponsor, mentor, and lift as they pursue their own talents can bring us great joy and satisfaction.

Focusing on serving the Savior can guide us toward making proper decisions in our daily lives. This perspective prepares us to do whatever the Lord may ask of us at any time. President Gordon B. Hinckley exemplified this important attitude. He said: "My talents may not be great, but I can use them to bless the lives of others. I can be one who does his work with pride in that which comes from hand and mind" ("Words of the Prophet: Put Your Shoulder to the Wheel," *New Era,* July 2000).

President Spencer W. Kimball said: "Let us remember, too, that greatness is not always a matter of the scale of one's life, but of the quality of one's life. True greatness is not always tied to the scope of our tasks, but to the quality of how we carry out our tasks whatever they are. In that attitude, let us give our time, ourselves, and our talents to the things that really matter now, things which will still matter a thousand years from now" ("First Presidency Message: A Gift of Gratitude," *Liahona,* December 1977).

President Thomas S. Monson said: "Expand your knowledge, both intellectual and spiritual, to the full stature of your divine potential. There is no limit to your influence for good. Share your talents, for that which we willingly share, we keep. But that which we selfishly keep, we lose" ("The Spirit of Relief Society," *Ensign,* May 1992).

Finally, *acknowledge God's hand in your success.* We must never forget or stop acknowledging that all talents and abilities come from God. Some were given to us before our birth, while others have been acquired as we have developed. However, in both cases, they are gifts from a benevolent Heavenly Father, whose gracious blessings are also the means for improving our talents and obtaining others. The Lord has said, "And in nothing doth man offend God, or against none is his wrath kindled, save those who confess not his hand in all things" (D&C 59:21).

Many years ago, Elder Marvin J. Ashton, a member of the Quorum of the Twelve, shared these powerful and inspiring words: "It pleases God to have us humbly recognize his powers and his influence in our accomplishments rather than to indicate by words or innuendo that we have been responsible for remarkable achievements" ("Neither Boast of Faith Nor of Mighty Works," *Ensign,* May 1990).

Elder Robert D. Hales, of the Quorum of the Twelve, counseled: "Prayer is an essential part of conveying appreciation to our Heavenly Father. He awaits our expressions of

*Elder Rasband with Elder Robert D. Hales,*
*general conference, October 2016.*

gratefulness each morning and night in sincere, simple prayer from our hearts for our many blessings, gifts, and talents" ("Gratitude for the Goodness of God," *Ensign,* May 1992).

It is my sincere hope that we will seriously ponder and pray to find our talents, that we may use them in building up the kingdom of God here on the earth, that we may be found worthy to stand before the Lord at the last day and in His presence hear Him say: "Well done, thou good and faithful servant: thou hast been faithful over a few things, I will make thee ruler over many things: enter thou into the joy of thy lord" (Matthew 25:21; see also 25:23).

We—as members of the Church, leaders of youth, anxious mothers and fathers, and concerned grandmothers and grandfathers—all need to respond to the call for "all hands on deck" as it pertains to our youth and young single adults. We must all look for opportunities to bless the youth whether or not we are currently closely associated with them. We must continue to teach and fortify fathers and mothers in their divinely declared roles with their children in the home. We must ask ourselves constantly if that extra sporting event, that extra activity or errand outside of the home is more important than families being together at home.

Now is the time when in every action we take, in every place we go, with every Latter-day Saint young person we meet, we need to have an increased awareness of the need for strengthening, nurturing, and being an influence for good in their lives.

# LOVING THE YOUTH

Not long after I was called into the Quorum of the Twelve in October 2015, I received an assignment that, frankly, terrified me. I was asked to join other Church leaders in a Face to Face broadcast with youth and their leaders and parents from around the world. I was told that more than 450,000 youth would be participating in this event as it was streamed live by internet. Questions would be asked in real time. How does one prepare for such an event? Never had I felt a greater need to depend on the Holy Ghost for guidance.

Our purpose was to introduce the Mutual theme for 2016, "Press forward with a steadfastness in Christ." The many hundreds of questions from the youth gave us an assurance that they truly wanted to do just that. Their questions were evidence of their desire to learn more, to draw closer to the Savior, and to strengthen their testimonies.

*Elder Rasband and young members of his family.*

The Spirit prompted me at one point to call upon my young family members, many of whom were in the audience that day, to come up and join me on the stand. Grandchildren, nieces, and nephews soon surrounded me. I told the audience, "This is my youth advisory council!"

Later feedback suggested that many youth were touched by that expression. They felt valued, that their contributions and opinions mattered, that they had a voice in the Church and in the family. That spontaneous action, instigated by the Spirit, was a blessing to many.

A similar occurrence a couple of years later showed yet again that the Lord has a hand in even small interactions. I was attending a mission presidents' seminar in Brazil when I learned of a large gathering of Latter-day Saint youth taking place simultaneously in many chapels all over the country.

I hadn't known of this event, and it was not on my agenda to attend, but I asked if I could join them in one of their locations. Adjustments were made to my schedule, a video link was quickly arranged, and I had a chance to speak to the youth and convey the love of the Brethren and of our Heavenly Father to them.

From far in the back, a young man held his hands up high and made the heart symbol with his hands. So I gave the heart symbol back from the pulpit.

*Elder Rasband at a Youth Meet-Up Event in Santos, Brazil.*

That simple, Spirit-directed action from that young man had a profound impact as thousands of youth all over Brazil lifted their hands in the heart symbol, adopting it as a symbol of unity and love for our Savior, Jesus Christ.

In something as simple as a gesture of the hands, the Spirit can work through us.

# LEADING US TO THE "ONE"

Throughout my life, I have come to know through my own experiences that Heavenly Father hears and answers our personal prayers. I know that Jesus is the living Christ and that He knows each of us individually, or as the scriptures express it, "one by one."

This sacred assurance is taught compassionately by the Savior Himself in His appearance to the people of Nephi. We read of this in 3 Nephi 11:15: "And it came to pass that the multitude went forth, and thrust their hands into his side, and did feel the prints of the nails in his hands and in his feet; and this they did do, going forth *one by one* until they had all gone forth" (emphasis added).

To further illustrate the "one by one" nature of our Savior's ministry, we read: "And it came to pass that when he had thus spoken, all the multitude, with one accord, did go forth with their sick and their afflicted, and their lame, and with their blind, and with their dumb, and with all them that were afflicted in any manner; and he did heal them *every one* as they were brought forth unto him" (3 Nephi 17:9; emphasis added).

We then read of the special blessing given to the precious children: "And when he had said these words, he wept, and the multitude bare record of it, and he took their little children, *one by one,* and blessed them, and prayed unto the Father for them" (3 Nephi 17:21; emphasis added).

This was not a small gathering. "And they were in number about two thousand and five hundred souls; and they did consist of men, women, and children." (3 Nephi 17:25).

Certainly, there is a very profound and tender personal message here. Jesus Christ ministers to and loves us all, one by one.

During the final months of our mission, we experienced an event that taught once again this profound principle that each of us is known and loved by God.

Elder Neal A. Maxwell was coming to New York City for some Church business, and we were informed that he would also like to have a mission conference. We were so pleased to have this opportunity to hear from one of the Lord's chosen servants. I was asked to select one of our missionaries to provide the opening prayer for the meeting. I might have randomly picked one of the missionaries to pray, but felt to ponder and prayerfully select one whom the Lord would have me ask.

In going through the missionary roster, a name boldly stood out to me: Elder Joseph Appiah of Accra, Ghana. He was the one I felt the Lord wanted to pray at the meeting.

Prior to the mission conference, I was having a regularly scheduled interview with Elder Appiah and told him of the prompting that I had received for him to pray. With amazement and humility in his eyes, he began to weep deeply. Somewhat surprised by his reaction, I started to tell him that it was all right and he wouldn't have to pray, when he informed me he would love to offer the prayer, that his emotion was caused by the love he has for Elder Maxwell. He told me that this Apostle is very special to the Saints in Ghana and to his own family. Elder Maxwell had called his father to be the district president in Accra and had sealed his mother and father in the Salt Lake Temple.

*Joseph Appiah, his wife, and their family with
Elder Rasband and son Christian Rasband.*

Now, I didn't know any of what I just related about this missionary or his family, but the Lord did, and He inspired a mission president on behalf of *one* missionary to provide a life-long memory and testimony-building experience.

At the meeting, Elder Appiah offered a wonderful prayer and made a humble contribution to a meeting where Elder Maxwell taught the missionaries of the attributes of Jesus Christ. All who were there will never forget the feelings of love they experienced for their Savior.

The title of the missionary manual
*Preach My Gospel* is taken from
Doctrine and Covenants 50:13–14, in which
the Lord asks this important question:
"Wherefore, I the Lord ask you this question—
unto what were ye ordained?
"To preach my gospel by the Spirit, even the
Comforter which was sent forth to teach the truth."

The First Presidency and Quorum of the Twelve
have been inspired to "raise the bar" for not
just missionaries, but really for all of us. The
entire Church is striving to rely more on
the promptings of the Holy Ghost.

# MISSIONARIES: CALLED BY THE SPIRIT

In June of 1837, the Prophet Joseph Smith called Heber C. Kimball, an Apostle, to go on a mission to England. Elder Kimball's call came as the two sat in the Kirtland Temple and Joseph spoke with divine authority: "Brother Heber, the Spirit of the Lord has whispered to me, 'Let my servant Heber go to England and proclaim my gospel and open the door of salvation to that nation'" (*Teachings of Presidents of the Church: Joseph Smith* [2007], 327).

That whispering of the Spirit is an example of how the call comes to servants of the Lord to send missionaries to their fields of labor. . . .

After finishing our mission assignment, I was called by President Gordon B. Hinckley to serve as a Seventy in the Church. Part of my early training as a new General Authority included an opportunity to sit with members of the Twelve as they assigned missionaries to serve in one of the hundreds of missions of this great Church.

With the encouragement and permission of President Henry B. Eyring, I would like to relate an experience, very special to me, which I had with him years ago when he was a member of the Quorum of the Twelve. Each Apostle holds the keys of the kingdom and exercises them at the direction and assignment of the President of the Church. Elder Eyring was assigning missionaries to their fields of labor, and as part of my training, I was invited to observe.

I joined Elder Eyring early one morning in a room where several large computer screens had been prepared for the session. There was also a staff member from the Missionary Department who had been assigned to assist us that day.

First, we knelt together in prayer. I remember Elder Eyring using very sincere words, asking the Lord to bless him to know "perfectly" where the missionaries should be assigned. The word "perfectly" said much about the faith that Elder Eyring exhibited that day.

As the process began, a picture of the missionary to be assigned would come up on one of the computer screens. As each picture appeared, to me it was as if the missionary were in the room with us. Elder Eyring would then greet the missionary with his kind and endearing voice: "Good morning, Elder X or Sister Y. How are you today?"

He told me that in his own mind he liked to think of where the missionaries would conclude their mission. This would aid him to know where they were to be assigned. Elder Eyring would then study the comments from the bishops and stake presidents, medical notes, and other issues relating to each missionary.

He then referred to another screen which displayed areas and missions across the world. Finally, as he was prompted by the Spirit, he would assign the missionary to his or her field of labor.

From others of the Twelve, I learned that this general method was typical each week as Apostles of the Lord assign scores of missionaries to serve throughout the world.

After assigning a few missionaries, Elder Eyring turned to me as he pondered one particular missionary and said, "So, Brother Rasband, where do you think this missionary should go?" I was startled! I quietly suggested to Elder Eyring that I did not know and that I did not know I could know! He looked at me directly and simply said, "Brother Rasband, pay closer attention and you too can know!" With that, I pulled my chair a little closer to Elder Eyring and the computer screen, and I did pay much closer attention!

A couple of other times as the process moved along, Elder Eyring would turn to me and say, "Well, Brother Rasband, where do you feel this missionary should go?" I would name a particular mission, and Elder Eyring would look at me thoughtfully and say, "No, that's not it!" He would then continue to assign the missionaries where he had felt prompted.

As we were nearing the completion of that assignment meeting, a picture of a certain missionary appeared on the screen. I had the strongest prompting, the strongest of the morning, that the missionary we had before us was to be assigned to Japan. I did not know that Elder Eyring was going to ask me on this one, but amazingly he did. I rather tentatively and humbly said to him, "Japan?" Elder Eyring responded immediately, "Yes, let's go there." And up on the computer screen the missions of Japan appeared. I instantly knew that the missionary was to go to the Japan Sapporo Mission.

Elder Eyring did not ask me the exact name of the mission, but he did assign that missionary to the Japan Sapporo Mission.

Privately in my heart I was deeply touched and sincerely grateful to the Lord for allowing me to experience the prompting to know where that missionary should go.

At the end of the meeting Elder Eyring bore his witness to me of the love of the Savior, which He has for each missionary assigned to go out into the world and preach the restored gospel. He said that it is by the great love of the Savior that His servants know where these wonderful young men and women, senior missionaries, and senior couple missionaries are to serve. I had a further witness that morning that every missionary called in this Church, and assigned or reassigned to a particular mission, is called by revelation from the Lord God Almighty through one of these, His servants.

I had occasion to be particularly grateful for this witness, and for the careful training I had received from Elder Eyring, when I was called to the Quorum of the Twelve and soon found myself in the position he had once occupied, working regularly to assign missionaries to their fields of labor. One such experience was especially noteworthy. I had assigned an elder to a mission in Russia, but as we continued moving down the list, I felt increasingly uneasy about it. We had assigned three more missionaries when I finally asked that we return to that elder.

Taking another look at his paperwork, I found nothing in the information from his bishop and stake president that would cause me to reconsider the assignment. Nor was there anything in his health or language history to suggest a change. But then my eye caught the information about his family, and I felt strongly impressed that this elder was to be assigned to teach the gospel in the country of his mother's ancestry. I made the reassignment and received the comforting assurance of the Spirit that the Lord's will had been done.

# A DIVINE "COINCIDENCE"

In 2017, I attended the twenty-year anniversary celebration of the Church meeting in Harlem. A five-story structure there now houses three wards and has become very much a community center for the people in that part of Manhattan.

The very weekend of the event, I had been assigned to a stake conference in New Jersey, across the Hudson River. When I learned of the gathering, I wanted to be there. Here's why:

In 1997, while I was mission president in the New York New York North Mission, I wrestled with how to find a meeting place for the growing membership in Harlem. These converts were coming to "a knowledge of the truth" (D&C 109:67), but they were having to go across town to worship. They needed a church in their own neighborhood where the spirit of the gospel could lift their hearts, where they could bring their friends and neighbors, where they could find peace

*Members gather in front of Sylvia's Restaurant in Harlem, 1997.*

and rest on the Sabbath, and where the love of God could pour out onto the streets.

One of our members stepped forward and offered his restaurant for our worship services. Sylvia's Restaurant was an icon in Harlem. We peered in the windows of Sylvia's to see if it would work. With it came more than seating—with it came confirmation that the Church had a place in the community. No question, when the Lord puts down roots in an area, the gospel thrives. It happened in Harlem and it is happening all over the world.

I believe it was by divine design that I was scheduled to be on the East Coast the weekend of the celebration, within driving distance and available for this momentous occasion. My

*The Church's current meetinghouse in Harlem.*

assignment had been made months before the event was announced, but the Lord knew I would want to be there. Clearly, He was blessing me with this opportunity to see the growth of the Church in an area so close to my heart and my stewardship.

TO BUILD FAITH

# AN ANSWER FROM
# THE SCRIPTURES

There was never any question in my mind that I would serve a mission. The only question I had was, "Where will I serve?" I thought I knew the answer. My dad went on a mission to Germany. My older brother went on a mission to Germany. My sister's boyfriend—and future husband—went on a mission to Germany. I thought I was going to Germany too. In fact, I planned on it.

When my mission call finally came, I was excited. I found a place where I could be alone and, despite my anticipation, slowly opened the envelope. "Dear Elder Ronald A. Rasband," I read. "You are hereby called to serve as a missionary for The Church of Jesus Christ of Latter-day Saints. You are assigned to labor in the Eastern States Mission."

The *Eastern States Mission*? I quickly scanned the letter for *Germany*, but it was not there. I had read the words correctly. I would not be going to a foreign country. I would not be learning German. I would not be walking the same streets as my father and brother. I would be serving stateside.

I'm glad family members weren't there recording the moment on their cell phones to post later on Facebook. (Of course, there were no cell phones or Facebook back then.) I was visibly disappointed and would have had a hard time faking excitement over my mission call. I took the call downstairs to my bedroom, knelt by my bed, and said a prayer. I needed a testimony that I was going to the mission Heavenly Father wanted me to go to. After praying, I randomly opened my scriptures. I wasn't really searching. I just needed an answer of some kind. As I opened my scriptures, I found myself in section 100 of the Doctrine and Covenants. I began reading the following verses:

"Behold, and lo, I have much people in this place, in the regions round about; and an effectual door shall be opened in the regions round about in this *eastern land*.

"Therefore, I, the Lord, have suffered you to come unto this place; for thus it was expedient in me for the salvation of souls" (D&C 100:3–4; emphasis added).

Immediately, the Holy Ghost confirmed to me that my assigned field of labor was no mistake. I went from being disappointed one minute to having the first of many spiritual impressions I would receive over the years. This strong spiritual impression confirmed to me that the Eastern States Mission

*Young Elder Rasband with missionary companions.*

was in fact where the Lord wanted me to serve. It was as if Heavenly Father was telling me, "Hey, Germany is not where I've called you. You're going to the 'eastern land.' So go there, open your mouth, and I will give you success." With that single spiritual experience, I changed my whole focus from being disappointed and wanting to be a missionary in Germany to knowing through the Holy Ghost that the Lord wanted me in the Eastern States Mission.

That was a pivotal experience in the building of my own faith—all thanks to the scriptures, the prompting I received to search them, and my mother for teaching me to love them.

# BUILDING BLOCKS OF
# FAITH AND TESTIMONY

As we are led by the Spirit, our personal journey through life provides us with many special experiences that become building blocks of faith and testimony. These experiences come to us in vastly different ways and at unpredictable times. They can be powerful spiritual events or small enlightening moments. Some experiences will come as serious challenges and heavy trials that test our ability to cope with them. No matter what the experience may be, each gives us a chance for personal growth, greater wisdom, and, in many cases, service to others with more empathy and love. As the Lord stated to the Prophet Joseph Smith in a reassuring way during one of his most significant trials at Liberty Jail, "All these things shall give thee experience, and shall be for thy good" (D&C 122:7).

As experiences accumulate in our lives, they add strength and support to each other. Just as the building blocks of our homes support the rest of the structure, so too do our personal life experiences become building blocks for our testimonies and add to our faith in the Lord Jesus Christ.

Think of the special experiences you have been blessed with in your life that have given you conviction and joy in your heart. Remember when you first knew that Joseph Smith was God's prophet of the Restoration? Remember when you accepted Moroni's challenge and knew that the Book of Mormon was indeed another testament of Jesus Christ? Remember when you received an answer to fervent prayer and realized that your Heavenly Father knows and loves you personally? As you contemplate such special experiences, don't they give you a sense of gratitude and resolve to go forward with renewed faith and determination?

Faith is increasing among God's covenant people, and I believe it is through having a personal treasury of such valued experiences that an increase of faith can happen for each of us.

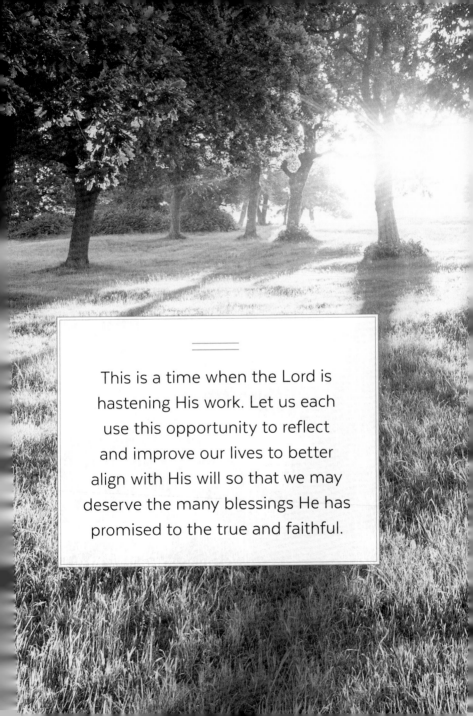

This is a time when the Lord is hastening His work. Let us each use this opportunity to reflect and improve our lives to better align with His will so that we may deserve the many blessings He has promised to the true and faithful.

# REMEMBER
# SPIRITUAL WITNESSES

Recall, especially in times of crisis, when you felt the Spirit and your testimony was strong; remember the spiritual foundations you have built. I promise that if you will do this, avoiding things that do not build and strengthen your testimony or that mock your beliefs, those precious times when your testimony prospered will return again to your memory through humble prayer and fasting. I assure you that you will once again feel the safety and warmth of the gospel of Jesus Christ.

All of us must first strengthen ourselves spiritually and then strengthen those around us. Ponder the scriptures regularly, and remember the thoughts and feelings you experience as you read them. Seek other sources of truth as well, but heed this caution from the scriptures: "But to be learned is good *if* they hearken unto the counsels of God" (2 Nephi 9:29; emphasis added). Attend Church meetings, especially sacrament meeting, and partake of the sacrament and renew covenants, including the promise to always remember the Savior, that His Spirit may ever be with you.

Never forget, question, or ignore personal, sacred spiritual experiences. The adversary's design is to distract us from spiritual witnesses, while the Lord's desire is to enlighten and engage us in His work.

Let me share a personal example of this truth. I distinctly recall a time when I received a prompting in answer to mighty prayer. The answer was clear and powerful. However, I failed to act immediately on the prompting, and after a period of time I began to wonder if what I had felt had been real. Some of you may have fallen for that deception of the adversary as well.

Several days later, I awoke with these powerful verses of scripture in my mind:

"Verily, verily, I say unto you, if you desire a further witness, cast your mind upon the night that you cried unto me in your heart. . . .

"Did I not speak peace to your mind concerning the matter? What greater witness can you have than from God?" (D&C 6:22–23).

It was as if the Lord was saying, "Now, Ronald, I already told you what you needed to do. Now do it!" How grateful I was for that loving correction and direction! I was immediately comforted by the prompting and was able to move forward, knowing in my heart that my prayer had been answered.

I share this experience to demonstrate how quickly our minds can forget and how spiritual experiences guide us. I have learned to cherish such moments "lest I forget."

I give you this promise: as you faithfully live the gospel of Jesus Christ and abide by its teachings, your testimony will be protected and it will grow. Keep the covenants you have made, regardless of the actions of those around you. Be diligent parents, brothers and sisters, grandparents, aunts, uncles, and friends who strengthen loved ones with personal testimony and who share spiritual experiences. Remain faithful and steadfast, even if storms of doubt invade your lives through the actions of others. Seek that which will edify and fortify you spiritually. Avoid counterfeit offerings of so-called "truths," which are so pervasive, and remember to record your feelings of "love, joy, peace, longsuffering, gentleness, goodness, faith, meekness, [and] temperance" (Galatians 5:22–23).

In the midst of life's greatest storms, *do not forget* your divine heritage as a son or daughter of God or your eternal destiny to one day return to live with Him, which will surpass anything the world has to offer. Remember the tender and sweet words of Alma: "Behold, I say unto you, my brethren, if ye have experienced a change of heart, and if ye have felt to sing the song of redeeming love, I would ask, can ye feel so now?" (Alma 5:26).

Questions are an indication of a further desire to learn, to add to those truths already in place in our testimonies, and to be better prepared to "press forward with a steadfastness in Christ" (2 Nephi 31:20).

The Restoration of the gospel began with a youth, Joseph Smith, asking a question. Many of the Savior's teachings in His ministry began with a question. Remember His question to Peter: "Whom say ye that I am?" (Matthew 16:15). And Peter's response: "Thou art the Christ, the Son of the living God" (Matthew 16:16). We need to help each other find Heavenly Father's answers through the guidance of the Spirit.

# FOLLOW RIGHTEOUS LEADERS

We sustain leaders who, by divine inspiration, have been called to teach and guide us and who are calling out to us to beware of the dangers we face each day—from casual Sabbath-day observance, to threats to the family, to assaults on religious freedom, and even to disputing latter-day revelation. Are we listening to their counsel?

Many times in conferences, sacrament meetings, and Primary we have sung the tender words, "Lead me, guide me, walk beside me" ("I Am a Child of God," *Hymns,* no. 301). What do those words mean to you? Who comes to mind when you think of them? Have you felt the influence of righteous leaders, those disciples of Jesus Christ who have helped you in the past and continue today to touch your life, who walk the Lord's path with you? They may be close at home. They may be in your local congregations or speaking from the pulpit at general conference. These disciples share with us the blessing of having a testimony of the Lord Jesus Christ, the leader of this Church, the leader of our very souls, who has promised, "Be of good cheer, and do not fear, for I the Lord am with you, and will stand by you" (D&C 68:6).

I stand as a witness of God the Eternal Father and His Son, Jesus Christ. I know our Savior lives and loves us and directs His servants, you and me, to fulfill His mighty purposes on this earth (see Mosiah 18:8–9).

As we press forward, choosing to follow the counsel and the warnings of our leaders, we choose to follow the Lord while the world is going in another direction. We choose to hold fast to the iron rod, to be Latter-day Saints, to be on the Lord's errand, and to be filled "with exceedingly great joy" (1 Nephi 8:12).

The growing question of today is clear: are you standing with the leaders of the Church in a darkening world so that you might spread the Light of Christ?

Relationships with leaders are so important and significant. No matter what age leaders may be, how close or far away, or when they may have touched our lives, their influence reflects the words of the American poet Edwin Markham, who said this:

> *There is a destiny that makes us brothers:*
> *[No one] goes his way alone:*

*All that we send into the lives of others*
*Comes back into our own.*
("A Creed," *Lincoln and Other Poems* [1901], 25).

When we reach out to lift one another, we prove those powerful words: "[No one] goes his way alone."

# STAND IN HOLY PLACES

Years ago, at the Logan Temple cornerstone ceremony in 1877, President George Q. Cannon said this: "Every foundation stone that is laid for a Temple, and every Temple completed . . . , lessens the power of Satan on the earth, and increases the power of God and Godliness, moves the heavens in mighty power in our behalf, invokes and calls down upon us the blessings of the Eternal Gods, and those who reside in their presence" ("The Logan Temple," *Millennial Star* 39, no. 46 [November 12, 1877]: 743).

Certainly in a day and time like we live in, the importance of every temple built and dedicated to the Lord cannot be overstated.

To what end and to what purpose is this focus, this emphasis on temple building? How does it apply to you? I am reminded of a passage of scripture that reads: "And again, I will give unto you a pattern in all things, that ye may not be deceived; for Satan is abroad in the land, and he goeth forth deceiving the nations" (D&C 52:14).

I would recommend that temple worship is an important pattern for each of you to set—individually and as families—as you consider your own areas of focus and attention, as you put in place firm foundations in your life.

The First Presidency has issued an invitation to all the members of the Church, which certainly applies to you and me: "Where time and circumstances permit, members are encouraged to replace some leisure activities with temple service. . . . All of the ordinances which take place in the House of the Lord become expressions of our belief in that fundamental and basic doctrine of the immortality of the human soul. As we redouble our efforts and our faithfulness in going to the temple, the Lord will bless us" (First Presidency letter, March 11, 2003; in "Encouraging Temple Worthiness and Preparation," *Ensign*, June 2003, and in *Ensign*, March 2004).

As we consider righteous patterns that we want to establish in our lives, we all would do well to continue remembering this admonition from the First Presidency. May we also consider the promised blessings by prophets, seers, and revelators as we faithfully attend the temple.

I would like to share a few of these promised blessings for our faithful service in the temple. First, from President Gordon B. Hinckley: "I would hope that we might go to the house of the Lord a little more frequently. . . . I encourage you to take greater advantage of this blessed privilege. It will refine your natures. It will peel off the selfish shell in which most of us live. It will literally bring a sanctifying element into our lives and make us better men and better women" ("Closing Remarks," *Ensign,* November 2004).

He also promised: "If there were more temple work done in the Church, there would be less of selfishness, less of contention, less of demeaning others. The whole Church would increasingly be lifted to greater heights of spirituality, love for one another, and obedience to the commandments of God" (*Teachings of Gordon B. Hinckley,* 622).

Now let me share a quote from President James E. Faust: "We unavoidably stand in so many unholy places and are subjected to so much that is vulgar, profane, and destructive of the Spirit of the Lord that I encourage our Saints all over the world, wherever possible, to strive to stand more often in holy places. Our most holy places are our sacred temples. Within them is a feeling of sacred comfort" ("Standing in Holy Places," *Ensign,* May 2005).

And from President Thomas S. Monson comes this promise: "Come to the temple and place your burdens before the Lord and you'll be filled with a new spirit and confidence in the future. Trust in the Lord, and if you do He'll hold you and cradle you and lead you step by step along that pathway that leads to the celestial kingdom of God" (quoted in Dell Van Orden, "San Diego Temple: 45th House of the Lord Dedicated in 'Season for Temple Building,'" *Church News,* May 8, 1993, Z8).

Another comforting blessing of temple worship is the assurance of protection and peace from the storm that is upon us in our day.

I think of a promise given in the Book of Mormon through Ammon in the book of Alma. Speaking of where members will be gathered into the garners, or temples of the Lord, he said: "Yea, they shall not be beaten down by the storm at the last day; yea, neither shall they be harrowed up by the whirlwinds; but when the storm cometh they shall be gathered together in their place, that the storm cannot penetrate to them; yea, neither shall they be driven with fierce winds whithersoever the enemy listeth to carry them" (Alma 26:6; see also verse 5).

Some of the safest places that Heavenly Father has established for the gathering of His people are in the temples of the Lord. I invite you to experience anew the feeling that you receive in these temples.

The way ahead will not be smooth or without incident. In the coming stages of your life you will feel the boat rocking under you, no matter your preparation or your sheer goodness. Recognize the turbulence for what it is. The Lord allows us challenges that at times will feel like tsunamis to make us strong and effective in His service and to help us always turn to Him.

# COME UNTO CHRIST

In order to be led by the Spirit, most of all, we need our Savior, our Lord, Jesus Christ. One of the accounts from scripture that has always spiritually moved me is when Jesus Christ walked out on the water to meet His disciples who were traveling in a ship on the Sea of Galilee. These were leaders newly called. The account is recorded in Matthew:

"But the ship was now in the midst of the sea, tossed with [the] waves: for the wind was contrary.

"And in the fourth watch of the night Jesus went unto them, walking on the sea.

"And when the disciples saw him walking on the sea, they were troubled, . . . and they cried out for fear.

"But straightway Jesus spake unto them, saying, Be of good cheer; it is I; be not afraid" (Matthew 14:24–27).

Peter heard that wonderful call of encouragement from the Lord.

"And Peter answered him and said, Lord, if it be thou, bid me come unto thee on the water.

"And [Jesus] said, Come" (Matthew 14:28–29).

Pretty bold. Peter was a fisherman, and he knew about the hazards of the sea. However, he was committed to following Jesus—night or day, on a ship or on dry land.

I can imagine that Peter leaped over the side of the boat, not waiting for a second invitation, and began to walk on the water. Indeed, the scripture says, "He walked on the water, to go to Jesus" (Matthew 14:29). As the wind increased in strength and force and as the waves swirled about his feet, Peter became "afraid; and beginning to sink, he cried [out], saying, Lord, save me.

"And immediately Jesus stretched forth his hand, and caught him" (Matthew 14:30–31).

Such a powerful lesson. The Lord was there for him, just as He is there for you and for me. He reached out His hand and drew Peter to Him and to safety.

I have needed the Savior and the rescue of His hand so many times. I need Him now as never before, as do you. I have felt confident at times leaping over the side of the boat, figuratively speaking, into unfamiliar places, only to realize that I could not do it alone.

You too will have your many moments to respond to frequent invitations to "come unto Christ" (Moroni 10:32). Isn't that what this mortal life is all about? The call may be to come rescue a family member; come help me answer my question; come serve a mission; come back to church; and come to the holy temple. In due time, each one of us will hear the call "Come home."

I pray that we will reach out—reach out and take the Savior's hand that He is extending to us, often through His divinely called leaders and our family members—and listen for His call to "Come."

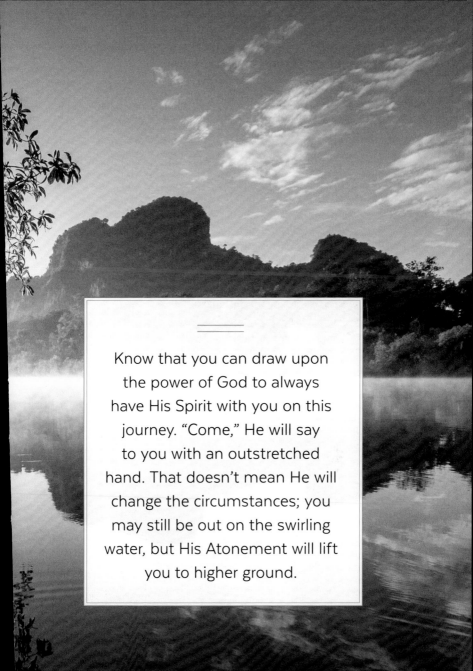

Know that you can draw upon the power of God to always have His Spirit with you on this journey. "Come," He will say to you with an outstretched hand. That doesn't mean He will change the circumstances; you may still be out on the swirling water, but His Atonement will lift you to higher ground.

DURING TIMES
OF TRIAL

# "PEACE BE UNTO THY SOUL"

It is not always easy to feel the influence of the Spirit when life is not going well. The Prophet Joseph Smith demonstrated this when, in March 1839, he and several of his companions had been wrongfully incarcerated for months at Liberty Jail. Many writers of Church history have said that this experience for the Prophet Joseph was certainly one of the most difficult and darkest periods of his entire life. His words "O God, where art thou?" (D&C 121:1) speak of a desperate loneliness in the bleakest of settings.

The Lord did not appear or send angels; He did not thrash the guards or swing wide the door of that damp, dirty cell. Put simply, He did not change the circumstances, but He spoke comfort and reassurance to Joseph like no other could: "My son, peace be unto thy soul; thine adversity and thine afflictions shall be but a small moment" (D&C 121:7). It was as if the Lord put His arm around Joseph when He said, "My son."

Those are precious and tender words. And then He put a time-table on Joseph's hardship—"a small moment." What a lesson for all of us to remember. Our hardships will be brief—in eternal terms—and the Lord will be right there.

Then the Lord said this: "Thy friends do stand by thee, and they shall hail thee again with warm hearts and friendly hands" (D&C 121:9).

Here was Joseph, locked in jail by the treachery of men, some of whom had once been his close associates. But the Lord made the point so clear—"thy friends do stand by thee." How comforting that declaration was to the Prophet Joseph; how comforting it is to us. Think for a minute what it means to you to know you have someone standing right by you, someone you can trust to be your friend on good days and bad, someone who values you and supports you even when the two of you are apart. In that regard, our most prized friend is Jesus Christ Himself.

The Lord's revelations are broad and far reaching for all in mortality. But each one of us—individually—has a place in the Lord's great plan of happiness. In small and seemingly simple ways He reaffirms that he is with us. He has promised, "I the Lord am with you and will stand by you" (D&C 68:6). That doesn't mean He changes our circumstances or even rights wrongs of everyday life. But He brings peace to us in troubled times and to fractured lives.

# SENT TO SUCCOR

In October 2017, a religious liberties conference was held in Sacramento, California, at which I was to deliver the keynote address. My participation had been planned many months in advance. But that weekend I learned another key reason that assignment had been made.

Earlier in the month, wildfires sweeping through Northern California had ravaged several neighborhoods in the area I was scheduled to visit. Many people had lost homes and possessions in the fires—for some, almost everything they owned was gone. There was an opportunity to include visits to some of these areas, and I immediately asked to have those ministering visits added to my schedule.

What a blessing it was to be with and try to bring comfort to those good people, along with Sister Joy D. Jones, General President of the Primary, and our spouses. It was a small miracle that we had been sent to the area at exactly this time.

Another small miracle was the fact that the Joneses had lived there in Sonoma County for more than a decade and knew many of the people we greeted.

I learned anew, in our meetings and interactions throughout the weekend, that God will often "call an audible," changing the purpose of an assignment at the last minute to accommodate the needs of His children. He loves each of them, and it was our privilege to share that love and concern by being with them personally in their time of distress. We felt the assurance of the Spirit that we had been sent there specifically at this time to comfort and bless them.

# PRESS ON AND TRUST GOD

One of the great examples of being led by the Spirit in trying times is the story of the Mormon handcart pioneers. Though they battled almost unimaginable adversities, they remained true and kept trusting God. Surely the Spirit led them through their difficulties.

A journal entry from that time told of that infamous hill in Church history called Rocky Ridge, where the Willie Handcart Company was out in Wyoming facing desperate times in an early winter. The words come from John Chislett, and the message comes from his heart, sanctified in the worst of times.

Chislett, age twenty-four, wrote:

> *A few days of bright freezing weather were succeeded by another snow storm. The day we crossed the Rocky Ridge it was snowing a little—the wind hard from the North West—and blowing so keenly that it almost pierced*

*us through. We had to wrap ourselves closely in blankets, quilts, or whatever else we could get, to keep from freezing. Captain Willie still attended to the details of the company's travelling, and this day he appointed me to bring up the rear.*

*My duty was to stay behind everything and see that nobody was left along the road. I had to bury a man who had died in my hundred, and I finished doing so after the company had started. In about half an hour, I set out on foot alone to do my duty as rear-guard to the camp. The ascent of the ridge commenced soon after leaving camp, and I had not gone far up it before I overtook a cart that the folks could not pull through the snow, here about knee-deep. I helped them along, and we soon overtook another.*

*By all hands getting to one cart we could travel; so we moved one of the carts a few rods, and then went back and brought up the other. After moving in this way for a while, we overtook other carts at different points of the hill, until we had six carts, not one of which could be moved by the parties owning it. I put our collective strength to three carts at a time, took them a short distance, and then brought up the other three. Thus by travelling over the hill three times—twice forward and once back—I succeeded after hours of toil in bringing my little company to the summit* (history.lds.org, Chislett, John, "Narrative," in T. B. H. Stenhouse, *The Rocky Mountain Saints: A Full and Complete History of the Mormons* [1873], 313–32).

Can you picture the scene? These were trail-weary pioneers—some in this very company were my own Moulton ancestors—wrapped in thin blankets to keep from freezing, and trudging in deep snow, exerting what little energy they had left to get to the top. I am sure it seemed insurmountable for them alone. However, Chislett came up from behind and added his strength and will to theirs, and then they picked up others along the way. Putting their "collective strength to three carts at a time," they were able to make the climb and eventually arrive at the evening fires: fires stoked by the sheer faith of the Saints. They had little else.

Many of you have in your youth recreated that trek experience out on a trail just to feel a small measure of what they felt as they followed the Lord's call to come to Zion. I doubt yours was in snow up to your knees, and yet that push and pull up the hill was still a staggering feat. How did you make it? How did they make it? "By travelling over the hill three times—twice forward and once back." The experience was truly an example of the second great commandment, "Thou shalt love thy neighbor as thyself" (Mark 12:31).

How does this apply to you? Let me suggest a few lessons to be learned from Chislett's account.

First, press on. Press on no matter how hard it gets, no matter how deep the snow, how steep the climb; no matter how little you have left to keep going. Remember and rely upon the Lord's promise, "Be of good cheer; I have overcome the world" (John 16:33).

You may be at the back of the pack like John Chislett. Recognize the responsibility to not leave anyone behind. There will be many you encounter with broken hearts and broken dreams. Lift them, help them move forward, boost their confidence in their ability, and renew their faith that the Lord is watching over them. He sent you.

The prophet Nephi taught: "Wherefore, ye must press forward with a steadfastness in Christ, having a perfect brightness of hope, and a love of God and of all men. Wherefore, if ye shall press forward, feasting upon the word of Christ, and endure to the end, behold, thus saith the Father: Ye shall have eternal life" (2 Nephi 31:20 ).

Pressing forward is a principle of righteousness in every dispensation. Let's look at the life of Nephi as an example.

This scripture, "Press forward with a steadfastness in Christ," comes after Lehi's family has reached the promised land. Like any trek—crossing the plains for the pioneers or crossing the desert and ocean for Lehi and company—it was hard going to get there. His brothers scorned Nephi for thinking he could take on Laban. And what did Nephi say? "Nevertheless I went forth" (1 Nephi 4:7). In other words, led by the Spirit, he pressed on.

You will have those who take issue with your determination to follow the will of the Lord. We see it all around us as attacks on religious freedom increase. Stay the course. Hold fast to the Lord's commandments—even in the face of challenges from unbelievers.

Nephi angered his brothers when he broke the steel bow he used to hunt for food. His brothers, at this point, had "hardened their hearts . . . , even unto complaining against the Lord their God" (1 Nephi 16:22). It was a pattern for them. Nephi made a bow out of wood, followed the directions of the pointers on the Liahona to the top the mountain, and there he slayed wild beasts. Led by the Spirit, he pressed on. It may not have been just how he wanted it, a wood bow in place of a fine steel one, hunting alone with no one at his side; however, he pressed on. You will be asked at times to do the same.

Nephi was commanded to build a ship and, though his brothers scorned his effort, he was successful, saying, "If God had commanded me to do all things I could do them. If he should command me that I should say unto this water, be thou earth, it should be earth; and if I should say it, it would be done" (1 Nephi 17:50).

Remember then that the family was out on the ship and the rebellious brothers tied him to the mast. They were busy making merry at first, but soon found themselves unable to steer the ship in a "terrible tempest" (1 Nephi 18:13). When it looked finally like they would be lost in the depths of the sea, the brothers loosed Nephi from his bindings. Said Nephi, "I did praise [God] all the day long; and I did not murmur against the Lord" (1 Nephi 18:16). Led by the Spirit, he pressed on, just as John Chislett did, and he carried his brothers forward with him every time. Will you?

You too will have moments when the adversary will come after you. He will make things hard or, sometimes worse, more alluring than living the commandments of God. Do not be drawn off or discouraged. Do not blame the Lord, for He has said, "I will make all my mountains a way, and my highways shall be exalted" (1 Nephi 21:11).

Trust Him. Pray for guidance, make a decision, and then take it to the Lord for His confirming peace. "When thou liest down at night lie down unto the Lord, that he may watch over you in your sleep; and when thou risest in the morning let thy heart be full of thanks unto God" (Alma 37:37).

If you find yourself in mists of darkness, get down on your knees. Brigham Young used to teach about prayer, "Knees get down, I say; and down bend the knees" (*Teachings of Presidents of the Church: Brigham Young* [1997], 45). It's that simple.

The Lord has a plan for each one of us, and He will unfold that plan as we turn to Him in prayer, seek His guidance, act upon His promptings, and press on.

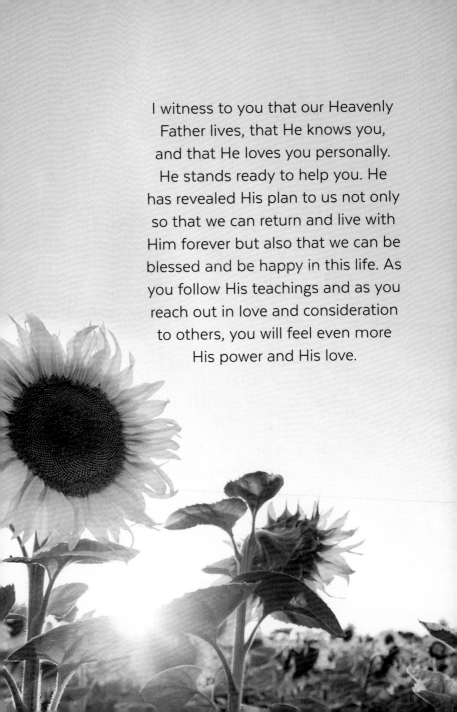

I witness to you that our Heavenly Father lives, that He knows you, and that He loves you personally. He stands ready to help you. He has revealed His plan to us not only so that we can return and live with Him forever but also that we can be blessed and be happy in this life. As you follow His teachings and as you reach out in love and consideration to others, you will feel even more His power and His love.

# "ANGELS ROUND ABOUT YOU, TO BEAR YOU UP"

On assignment one day in Oklahoma, I had the opportunity to meet with a few of the families devastated by mighty twisters that had recently swept through that area. As I visited with the Sorrels family, I was particularly touched by the experience of their daughter, Tori, then a fifth grader at Plaza Towers Elementary School.

Tori and a handful of her friends huddled in a restroom for shelter as the tornado roared through the school. Here is Tori's account of that day:

"I heard something hit the roof. I thought it was just hailing. The sound got louder and louder. I said a prayer that Heavenly Father would protect us all and keep us safe. All of a sudden we heard a loud vacuum sound, and the roof disappeared right above our heads. There was lots of wind and debris flying around and hitting every part of my body. It was darker outside and it looked like the sky was black, but it wasn't—

*Elder Rasband in Moore, Oklahoma, at destroyed elementary school.*

it was the inside of the tornado. I just closed my eyes, hoping and praying that it would be over soon.

"All of a sudden it got quiet.

"When I opened my eyes, I saw a stop sign right in front of my eyes! It was almost touching my nose" (Experience of Victoria [Tori] Sorrels, recounted January 16, 2014). Tori, her mother, three of her siblings, and numerous friends who were also in the school with her miraculously survived that tornado; seven of their schoolmates did not.

That weekend the priesthood brethren gave many blessings to members who had suffered in the storm. I was humbled to give Tori a blessing. As I laid my hands on her head, a favorite scripture came to mind: "I will go before your face. I will be on your right hand and on your left, and my Spirit shall be in your hearts, and mine angels round about you, to bear you up" (D&C 84:88).

I counseled Tori to remember the day when a servant of the Lord laid his hands on her head and pronounced that she had been protected by angels in the storm.

Many times in my own life I have felt an assurance that God is interested in me—in my personal salvation. And as Moses knew (Moses 1:6), I know that I am one of Heavenly Father's sons. I also know that each of us is precious to and loved by God. He cares, He whispers, and He watches over us in ways unique to each of our lives.

Like Nephi of old, I can say: "I do not know the meaning of all things" (1 Nephi 11:17). Nevertheless, I do know and witness that God our Father and His Son, Jesus Christ, in their infinite greatness, know and love you and me personally.

# SPECIAL LESSONS TO LEARN

Little Paxton, our grandson, was born with a very rare chromosomal deletion, a genetic disorder that distinguishes him, literally, as one in hundreds of millions. For our daughter and her husband, an uncharted, life-changing journey began when Paxton was born. This experience has become a crucible for learning special lessons tied to the eternities.

President Russell M. Nelson taught: "For reasons usually unknown, some people are born with physical limitations. Specific parts of the body may be abnormal. Regulatory systems may be out of balance. And all of our bodies are subject to disease and death. Nevertheless, the gift of a physical body is priceless. . . .

"A perfect body is not required to achieve a divine destiny. In fact, some of the sweetest spirits are housed in frail frames. . . .

"Eventually the time will come when each 'spirit and . . . body shall be reunited again in . . . perfect form; both limb

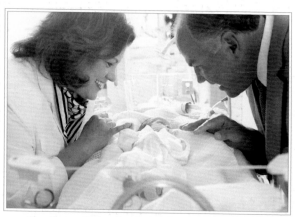

*Grandma and Grandpa Rasband with newborn Paxton.*

and joint shall be restored to its proper frame' (Alma 11:43). Then, thanks to the Atonement of Jesus Christ, we can become perfected in Him" ("We Are Children of God," *Ensign,* November 1998).

To all of you who have challenges, concerns, disappointments, or heartaches with a dear one, know this: with infinite love and everlasting compassion, God our Heavenly Father loves your afflicted one, and He loves you!

Some might ask when faced with such suffering, how could Almighty God let this happen? And then that seemingly inevitable question, why did this happen to me? Why must we experience disease and events that disable or call precious family members home early or extend their years in pain? Why the heartaches?

At these moments we can turn to the great plan of happiness authored by our Heavenly Father. That plan, when presented in the pre-earth life, prompted us all to shout for joy (see Job 38:7). Put simply, this life is training for eternal exaltation, and that process means tests and trials. It has always been so, and no one is spared.

Trusting in God's will is central to our mortality. With faith in Him, we draw upon the power of Christ's Atonement at those times when questions abound and answers are few. The Spirit can lead us to the peace we need.

After His Resurrection, when visiting the Americas, our Savior, Jesus Christ, reached out to all with this invitation:

"Have ye any that are sick among you? Bring them hither. Have ye any that are lame, or blind, or halt, or maimed, or leprous, or that are withered, or that are deaf, or that are afflicted in any manner? Bring them hither and I will heal them, for I have compassion upon you; my bowels are filled with mercy. . . .

"And it came to pass that when he had thus spoken, all the multitude, with one accord, did go forth with their sick and their afflicted, and their lame, and with their blind, and with their dumb, and with all them that were afflicted in any manner; and he did heal them every one as they were brought forth unto him" (3 Nephi 17:7, 9).

Great strength can be found in the words "all the multitude . . . did go forth"—*all*. We *all* face challenges. And then the phrase: "that were afflicted in any manner." All of us can identify, can't we?

Shortly after precious Paxton was born, we knew Heavenly Father would bless us and teach us special lessons. As his father and I put our fingers on his tiny head in the first of many priesthood blessings, the words came into my mind from the ninth chapter of John: "that the works of God should be made manifest in him" (John 9:3).

God's works are definitely being made manifest through Paxton.

We have learned patience, faith, and gratitude through the balm of service, endless hours of intense emotions, tears of empathy, and the prayers and expressions of love for dear ones in need, especially Paxton and his parents.

President James E. Faust, my boyhood stake president, said: "I have a great appreciation for those loving parents who stoically bear and overcome their anguish and heartbreak for a child who was born with or who has developed a serious mental or physical infirmity. This anguish often continues every day, without relief, during the lifetime of the parent or the child. Not infrequently, parents are required to give superhuman nurturing care that never ceases, day or night. Many a mother's arms and heart have ached years on end, giving

*Paxton Edward Norton at age fifteen months.*

comfort and relieving the suffering of her special child" ("The Works of God," *Ensign,* November 1984).

As described in Mosiah, we have witnessed the Savior's pure love given to Paxton's family, which love is available to all: "And now it came to pass that the burdens which were laid upon Alma and his brethren were made light; yea, the Lord did strengthen them that they could bear up their burdens with ease, and they did submit cheerfully and with patience to all the will of the Lord" (Mosiah 24:15).

One night early in Paxton's life, we were in the neonatal intensive care unit of the wonderful Primary Children's Medical Center in Salt Lake City, Utah, marveling at the dedicated, undivided attention given by the doctors, nurses, and caregivers. I asked my daughter how we would ever pay for this and ventured a guess at what the cost would be. A doctor standing nearby suggested that I was "way low" and that little Paxton's care would cost substantially more than I had estimated. We learned that much of the expense for care given in this hospital is covered by the generous gifts of time and monetary contributions of others. His words humbled me as I thought of the worth of this tiny little soul to those who were so carefully watching over him.

I was reminded of a familiar missionary scripture that took on new meaning: "Remember the worth of souls is great in the sight of God" (D&C 18:10). I wept as I pondered the limitless love our Heavenly Father and His Beloved Son, Jesus Christ, have for each one of us, while learning in a powerful way what the worth of a soul is, both physically and spiritually, to God.

Paxton's family learned they are surrounded by countless heavenly and earthly ministering angels. Some quietly slipped in when needed and silently slipped out. Others were at the door with food, doing the laundry, picking up the siblings, calling with encouragement, and especially praying for Paxton. Thus another special lesson learned: If you come upon a person who is drowning, would you ask if they need help—or would it be better to just jump in and save them from the deepening waters? The offer, while well meaning and often given, "Let me know if I can help," is really no help at all.

We continue to learn the important value of being aware of and interested in the lives of those around us, learning not only the importance of giving help but also the overwhelming joy that comes from helping others.

President Thomas S. Monson, who was such a magnificent example of lifting the downtrodden, said: "God bless all who endeavor to be their brother's keeper, who give to ameliorate suffering, who strive with all that is good within them to make a better world. Have you noticed that such individuals have a brighter smile? Their footsteps are more certain. They have an aura about them of contentment and satisfaction . . . for one cannot participate in helping others without experiencing a rich blessing himself" ("Our Brothers' Keepers," *Ensign,* June 1998).

Though we will face trials, adversities, disabilities, heartaches, and all manner of afflictions, our caring, loving Savior will always be there for us. He has promised:

"I will not leave you comfortless: I will come to you. . . .

"My peace I give unto you: not as the world giveth, give I unto you. Let not your heart be troubled, neither let it be afraid" (John 14:18, 27).

How grateful we are to our Father in Heaven for our champion Paxton. Through him the Lord has manifest His works and continues to teach us these valuable, sacred, and special lessons.

RECOGNIZING HIS
HAND IN OUR LIVES

# BY DIVINE DESIGN

Do you remember the story of Alma leaving Ammonihah due to the wickedness of the people? Soon an angel appeared to Alma and called him to "return to the city of Ammonihah, and preach again unto the people of the city" (Alma 8:16).

Alma did so "speedily," entering "the city by another way" (Alma 8:18).

"As he entered the city he was an hungered, and he said to a man: Will ye give to an humble servant of God something to eat?

"And the man said unto him: I am a Nephite, and I know that thou art a holy prophet of God, for thou art the man whom an angel said in a vision: Thou shalt receive" (Alma 8:19–20).

The man was Amulek.

Now, did Alma just happen upon Amulek? No, it was no coincidence that he went into the city by the way that would lead him to this faithful man who would become his missionary companion.

Elder Neal A. Maxwell once explained: "None of us ever fully utilizes the people-opportunities allocated to us within our circles of friendship. You and I may call these intersectings 'coincidence.' This word is understandable for mortals to use, but *coincidence* is not an appropriate word to describe the workings of an omniscient God. He does not do things by 'coincidence' but . . . by 'divine design'" ("Brim with Joy," Brigham Young University devotional, January 23, 1996, speeches.byu.edu).

Our lives are like a chessboard, and the Lord moves us from one place to another—if we are responsive to spiritual promptings. Looking back, we can see His hand in our lives.

We can see such heavenly intervention in the story of when Nephi returned to get the plates from Laban. He "was led by the Spirit, not knowing beforehand the things [that he] should do" (1 Nephi 4:6). Laban was soon before him in a drunken stupor, and Nephi slew him, retrieved the plates, and fled back to his brothers. Was he fortunate to just happen upon Laban? Or was it by "divine design"?

Significant events unfold in the gospel and in the Church that further the kingdom of God on earth. They are not by accident but by God's plan. He who fashioned this world can calm the seas with His word and can steer both Alma and Amulek and Nephi and Laban to be at the right place at precisely the right time.

Likewise, events and associations unfold in each of our lives that further God's work on earth.

Elder Joseph B. Wirthlin spoke of an occasion when President Thomas S. Monson said to him: "There is a guiding hand above all things. Often when things happen, it's not by accident. One day, when we look back at the seeming coincidences of our lives, we will realize that perhaps they weren't so coincidental after all" ("Lessons Learned in the Journey of Life," *Ensign,* December 2000).

Most often, our good works are known to only a few. They are, however, recorded in heaven. One day, we will stand as a witness of our whole-souled devotion to works of righteousness. No trial or calamity can derail God's plan of happiness. Indeed, by "divine design," "joy cometh in the morning" (Psalm 30:5). "I came into the world to do the will of [the] Father" (3 Nephi 27:13), Jesus taught. So did we.

Through the experience of my own life's journey, I know that the Lord will move us on that seeming chessboard to do His work. What may appear to be a random chance is, in fact, overseen by a loving Father in Heaven, who can number the hairs of every head (see Luke 12:7). Not even a sparrow falls to the ground without our Father's notice (see Matthew 10:29). The Lord is in the small details of our lives, and those incidents and opportunities are to prepare us to lift our families and others as we build the kingdom of God on earth. Remember, as the Lord said to Abraham, "I know the end from the beginning; therefore my hand shall be over thee" (Abraham 2:8).

# THE LORD'S INVOLVEMENT

The Lord placed me in a home with loving parents. By the world's standards, they were very ordinary people: my father, a devoted man, was a truck driver; my angel mother, a stay-at-home mom. The Lord helped me find my lovely wife, Melanie; He prompted a businessman, who became a dear friend, to give me an employment opportunity. The Lord called me to serve in the mission field, both as a young man and as a mission president; He called me to the Quorum of the Seventy; and now He has called me as an Apostle. Looking back, I realize I did not orchestrate any of those moves; the Lord did, just as He is orchestrating important moves for you and for those you love.

What should you be looking for in your own life? What are God's miracles that remind you that He is close, saying, "I am right here"? Think of those times, some daily, when the Lord has acted in your life—and then acted again. Treasure them as moments the Lord has shown confidence in you and in your choices. But allow Him to make more of you than you can make of yourself on your own. Treasure His involvement.

Sometimes we consider changes in our plans as missteps on our journey. Think of them more as first steps to being "on the Lord's errand" (D&C 64:29).

# "CHANCE" MEETINGS

Some time ago our granddaughter joined a youth group to tour several Church history sites. The final itinerary noted that she would be passing through the very area where her missionary brother, our grandson, was serving. Our granddaughter had no intention of seeing her brother on his mission. However, as the bus entered the town where her brother was serving, two missionaries could be seen walking down the street. One of the missionaries was her brother.

Anticipation filled the bus as the youth asked the bus driver to pull over so she could greet her brother. In less than one minute, after tears and sweet words, her brother was back on his way to fulfill his missionary duties. We later learned that her brother had been on that street for less than five minutes, walking from an appointment to his car.

*Rasband grandchildren in Rutland, Vermont.*

Heavenly Father can put us in situations with specific intent in mind. He has done so in my life, and He is doing so in yours, as He did in the lives of our dear grandchildren.

Over a year ago, as I was walking through Temple Square, one of the sister missionaries approached me and asked, "Do you remember me? I am from Florida." She told me her name, Sister Aida Chilan. Yes, I remembered meeting her and her family. Her stake president had suggested we visit her family. It became apparent that we were there for their daughter Aida, who had not been baptized. After our visit and more than a year of teaching and fellowshipping, Aida was baptized.

After we visited on Temple Square, she wrote me a letter. She said: "I know with all my heart that Heavenly Father

*Elder Rasband with Sister Chilan and Sister Mou.*

knows each of us and that He continues to place us in each other's paths for a reason. Thank you for being one of my missionaries, for reaching out to me and finding me five years ago" (Letter from Aida Chilan, April 20, 2017). Aida also sent me her conversion story recounting the "divine coincidences" in her life that led to her baptism and confirmation, her serving a mission on Temple Square, and her recent temple marriage (Letter from Aida Chilan, May 30, 2017).

Was it a mere coincidence that the stake president had steered us to the Chilan home or that she and I would later meet on Temple Square? Aida's testimony bears record that this was all part of God's "divine design."

We all have similar things happen in our lives. We may meet someone who seems familiar, renew an acquaintance, or find common ground with a stranger. When those occur, perhaps the Lord is reminding us that we are all truly brothers and sisters. We are really engaged in the same cause—in what Joseph Smith called "the cause of Christ" (*Teachings of Presidents of the Church: Joseph Smith* [2007], 352).

Each of us is precious and loved by the Lord, who cares, who whispers, and who watches over us in ways unique to each of us. He is infinitely wiser and more powerful than mortal men and women. He knows our challenges, our triumphs, and the righteous desires of our hearts.

# THE ROLE OF AGENCY

Now, where does our agency fit in a "divine design"? We have a choice to follow or to not follow our Savior and His chosen leaders. The pattern is clear in the Book of Mormon when the Nephites had turned away from the Lord. Mormon lamented:

"And they saw . . . that the Spirit of the Lord did no more preserve them; yea, it had withdrawn from them because the Spirit of the Lord doth not dwell in unholy temples—

"Therefore the Lord did cease to preserve them by his miraculous and matchless power, for they had fallen into a state of unbelief and awful wickedness" (Helaman 4:24–25).

Not all that the Lord asks of us is a result of how strong we are, how faithful we are, or what we may know. Think of Saul, whom the Lord stopped on the road to Damascus. He was going the wrong direction in his life, and it had nothing to do with north or south. Saul was divinely redirected. When he was known later as Paul, his apostolic ministry reflected what the Lord already knew he was capable of doing and becoming, not what he had set out to do as Saul. In the same manner, the Lord knows what each of us is capable of doing and becoming. What did the Apostle Paul teach? "And we know that all things work together for good to them that love God, to them who are the called according to his purpose" (Romans 8:28).

When we are righteous, willing, and able, when we are striving to be worthy and qualified, we progress to places we never imagined and become part of Heavenly Father's divine design. All of us have divinity within us. When we see God working through us and with us, may we be encouraged, even grateful for that guidance. When our Father in Heaven said, "This is my work and my glory—to bring to pass the immortality and eternal life of man" (Moses 1:39), He was talking about all of His children—you in particular.

The Lord's hand is guiding you. By divine design, He is in the small details of your life as well as the major milestones. As it says in Proverbs, "Trust in the Lord with all thine heart; . . . and he shall direct thy paths" (Proverbs 3:5–6). He will bless you, sustain you, and bring you peace.

# PHOTO CREDITS

vi: Alta Oosthuizen/Shutterstock.com

2: www.fredconcha.com/Moment/ Getty Images

5: Alex Yuzhakov/Shutterstock.com

6: aniszewski/iStock/Getty Images

8: Courtesy of the Rasband family

9: Courtesy of the Rasband family

11: borchee/iStock/Getty Images

12: georgeolsson/E+/Getty Images

15: Marco Bottigelli/Shutterstock.com

16: SNEHIT/Shutterstock.com

18: Courtesy of the Rasband family

20: EpicStockMedia/Shutterstock.com

22: Simon Gakhar/Moment/Getty Images

26: Photos by R A Kearton/Moment/ Getty Images

28: Bartfett/iStock/Getty Images

31: duncan1890/DigitalVision Vectors/ Getty Images

35: Image by Chris Winsor/Moment/ Getty Images

36: Thang Tat Nguyen/Moment/Getty Images

39: Image by Chris Winsor/Moment/ Getty Images

40: Portra/DigitalVision/Getty Images

42: Dave and Les Jacobs/Blend Images/ Getty Images

45: Courtesy of the Rasband family

47: Robert Daly/OJO Images/Getty Images

48: RichVintage/E+/Getty Images

50: Courtesy of the Rasband family

52: Photo by Malina Grigg

55: AGrigorjeva/iStock/Getty Images

56: mrPliskin/E+/Getty Images

58: 24Novembers/Shutterstock.com

61: Dave and Les Jacobs/Blend Images/ Getty Images

62: Cantemir Olaru/Shutterstock.com

64: Courtesy of the Rasband family

66: RayTango/iStock/Getty Images

69: Twinsterphoto/Shutterstock.com

70: AGrigorjeva/iStock/Getty Images

72: Jacek_Sopotnicki/iStock/Getty Images

74: Auxins/iStock/Getty Images

77: Courtesy of the Rasband family

80: Photo courtesy The Office of the President

82: Witthaya Prasongsin/EyeEm/ Getty Images

84: Jasmina007/iStock/Getty Images

86: Photo by Melanie T. Rasband

87: Photo courtesy Brazil Area Office

88: Christiana Stawski/Moment Open/ Getty Images

91: Courtesy of the Rasband family

93: Sandy Potere/EyeEm/Getty Images

94: Carolin Voelker/Moment Open/ Getty Images

100: Natali_Giglavaya/Shutterstock.com

102: Courtesy of the Rasband family

103: Courtesy of the Rasband family

104: Manuel Breva Colmeiro/Moment/ Getty Images

106: Radius Images/Radius Images/ Getty Images

109: Courtesy of the Rasband family

110: David Fenton/EyeEm/Getty Images

113: Nick Brundle Photography/ Moment/Getty Images

114: Trifonov_Evgeniy/iStock/Getty Images

118: PrimePhoto/Shutterstock.com

120: Biletskiy_Evgeniy/iStock/Getty Images

124: Altus Photo Design/Moment/Getty Images

129: Nejron Photo/Shutterstock.com

130: Richard Fairless/Moment/Getty Images

134: Dulyanut Swdp/Moment/Getty Images

136: john finney photography/Moment/ Getty Images

138: Evgeni Dinev Photography/ Moment/Getty Images

141: Jacob_09/Shutterstock.com

142: Dmytro Gilitukha/Shutterstock.com

145: Andris Tkacenko/Shutterstock.com

146: holicow/E+/Getty Images

153: Getman/Shutterstock.com

154: solarseven/Shutterstock.com

156: Courtesy of the Rasband family

158: Kiyoshi Hijiki/Moment/Getty Images

160: Ins Dias/EyeEm/Getty Images

162: Courtesy of the Rasband family

165: Courtesy of the Rasband family

168: zlikovec/Shutterstock.com

170: Lane V. Erickson/Shutterstock.com

174: borchee/iStock/Getty Images

177: vulcano/Shutterstock.com

178: Grisha Bruev/Shutterstock.com

180: Courtesy of the Rasband family

181: Courtesy of the Rasband family

183: abinkung/Shutterstock.com

184: fotohunter/Shutterstock.com

Background: VolodymyrSanych/ Shutterstock.com